Fun with Nan and Pop!

by Vaishali Batra

OXFORD
UNIVERSITY PRESS
AUSTRALIA & NEW ZEALAND

We get on a bus.

It will be fun with them!

We go to the shops.

We pack a bag.

I will get the rug.

We sit on the rug.

We rush to check the bugs.

We dig.

Then we fill a bucket.

We sit on a rock.

13

We chat.

We nap!